31 Steps to a Better YouTube Channel

Philip Vang

Contents

Contents

1 Introduction

I want to thank you and congratulate you for getting the book, "31 Steps to a Better YouTube Channel: Optimize Your Channel, Make More Money, Gain Subscribers, Audience and Views. This Ultimate Guide Will Help You To Make A Living of YouTube".

With this book, you will learn how to setup or improve the quality of your YouTube Channel, gain more subscribers and eventually be able to make money doing videos on YouTube. This will be an epic journey and I hope to have some valuable steps here.

Thanks again for getting this book, I hope you enjoy it!

Sincerely,

Philip Vang

Author of 31 Steps to a Better YouTube Channel

2 Publisher's Note

Care has been taken to confirm the accuracy of the information presented and to describe generally accepted practices. However, the authors, editors, and publisher are not responsible for errors or omissions or for any consequences from application of the information in this book and make no warranty, express or implied, with respect to the contents of the publication.

The authors, editors, and publisher have exerted every effort to ensure that any drug selection and dosage set forth in this text are in accordance with current recommendations and practice at the time of publication. However, in view of ongoing research, changes in government regulations, and the constant flow of information relating to drug therapy and drug reactions, the reader is urged to check the package insert for each drug for any change in indications and dosage and for added warnings and precautions. This is particularly important when the recommended agent is a new or infrequently employed drug.

Some drugs and medical devices presented in this publication may have Food and Drug Administration (FDA) clearance for limited use in restricted research settings. It is the responsibility of the health care provider to ascertain the FDA status of each drug or device planned for use in their clinical practice.

Google and the Google logo are registered trademarks of Google Inc., used with permission.

YouTube and the YouTube logo are registered trademarks of Google Inc., used with permission.

3 Step 1: Sign Up for an Account on YouTube

YouTube has this thing called "open-door policy", in which any-one who goes to the website can have an access to the content of the site. You are not required to register to be able to browse and watch videos. However, if you want to use YouTube in ways other than merely watching other people's videos, then it is better to open an account.

Signing up for a YouTube account is not complicated at all since YouTube does not require you to give out lots of information. It t does not even ask for your home address or telephone number. If you would compare it to other sites, YouTube registration is apparently non-intrusive. Moreover, you can use your Gmail account to set up a YouTube channel. Just click on either the Upload or Sign In buttons on the upper right hand corner of the page that will prompt you to sign in using your email account.

4 Step 2: Choose an Appropriate Username

Your username will be your channel's identity. In fact, people will most likely recognize you through your username rather than your own name.

When it comes to choosing a username, one of the most important things to keep in mind is that it must be able to capture the entirety of your channel and carry your identity as a YouTuber. For instance, if your videos are about music, then you may want to connect your username with music. Some people also opt to use their real name as their username, since they want to get their names out there. They want to be known as themselves. Whatever your choice of username is, make sure that it is professional enough and that it will not give people the impression that you are not worth it.

5 Step 3: Familiarize Yourself With Your Channel

So now, you already have your YouTube account. You can do several things that only registered users can do, such as like or dislike a video, comment on it, flag it as inappropriate, and so on. Moreover, it means that you already have your own channel where you can upload your videos.

After you log in your account, you can access your channel by clicking the button right next to the YouTube logo. Just click the My Channel button on the dropdown menu and this will redirect you to your channel, where you can browse through your videos (if you have already uploaded one), create playlists, and do more.

It is important to familiarize yourself with your channel. Of course, you will be using it for as long as you are on YouTube. Know where you can access the videos, the subscriptions, and others.

6 Step 4: Customize Your Channel

Statistically speaking, people tend to trust accounts that are organized (i.e. those that have decent picture and username) rather than those that aren't. Therefore, after signing up for an account, it is also important to customize your channel.

Add a decent profile picture so people will know that you are legitimate. YouTube also now lets you upload a banner, known as the channel art, which helps brand the identity of your channel, and give it a unique appearance as well as feel. If you want to add a channel art, then you just have to click the Add channel art button, which is located within the banner placeholder on top of the YouTube page. If you already have a channel art and you just want to change it, hover the mouse on the channel art and click on the edit icon that will appear and click Edit channel art.

7 Step 5: Set Your Channel Preferences

Sometimes, it is inevitable to change your mind. There will come a time when you are no longer interested in the username that you have chosen the moment you created your YouTube account, or you might have just come up with a better username than the one you are currently using.

The good thing about YouTube is that it lets you do all the changes that you want. You can change your username, your email address, your password-practically anything. If you want to modify the settings of your YouTube channel, just click on your picture on the upper right hand corner of the page (which is beside the Notifications icon-the bell-like icon), and then click on the Settings button (the gear-like icon). You will then be redirected to the settings page where you can change your name, password, email, and other additional features.

8 Step 6: Write a Description About Your Channel

Since you are still new, it is most likely that people still do not have any idea what your channel is really all about. You still have to give people a clear idea as to what it has to offer.

That being said, it is necessary to write a description about your channel. You can do so by going to your channel, clicking the About tab, and then clicking the Channel Description button. A text box will appear and this is where you will put the description. Afterwards, the description will then appear when people go to the About section of your channel. Keep in mind that the description must be able to give people a clear overview of what your channel is all about and what it has to offer. It must also be interesting and impressive enough to convince people to give you a shot.

9 Step 7: Browse for Other Channels on the Channels Page

People on YouTube - even the most popular ones - do not get subscribers in an instant. Of course, they have to start with zero subscribers, then one, two, and so on until they already have a million subscribers and channel views. Since you just started your channel, you cannot expect that people will already notice you. Other channels on YouTube are still likely to overshadow you.

Connecting to other people on YouTube is one of the basic things that you can do to get noticed. You can start by browsing other YouTube channels, most especially those related to your channel. To explore other YouTube channels, you can go the Channels page (www.youtube.com/channels) or click on the Browse Channel, which you can find at the lowest part of the drop-down menu beside the YouTube logo.

10 Step 8: Subscribe to Other People's Channels

As you browse for channels on YouTube, it is most likely that you will come across some great ones. These are the ones that you want to visit again next time.

If you want to keep track of the channels that you like, then you must subscribe to them. You will no longer have to search for their channels since your subscriptions will already be added to the Subscriptions section of your channel. You will just have to click on their channel among the list of your subscriptions.

Another perk of subscribing to a channel is that you will also receive a notification every time a new video is uploaded on that channel. These new videos will appear in the Your Subscriptions section on the home page of YouTube once you log in. Don't worry; subscribing to a channel is just one click away.

11 Step 9: Leave Comments on Other YouTuber's Videos

When you watch a video on YouTube, there are times when you feel that you just have to leave a comment on that video. It may be because that video is so good that you feel like you really have to tell the uploader "good job". It may also be because the video is thought provoking and it calls for a discussion.

Leaving a comment on some videos is one way of connecting with other YouTubers. It is like stepping out of your shell and telling people "Hey, I have a channel, too!" Who knows, this is also your chance to get noticed by other people on YouTube, which in turn can help you gain more subscribers. This is most especially true if you have an interesting username that will convince people to look at your channel.

12 Step 10: Send Messages to Other People on YouTube

Aside from leaving comments on other people's videos, one way to get in touch with them is by sending them messages. Some people may not be aware of this, but yes, you can send private messages to other people on YouTube! It is just like what you do in any other social networking sites (YouTube is basically a social networking site). All you have to do is to visit that person's channel and then click on the About tab. Afterwards, click the Send Message button, type in your message, and then click Send. On the other hand, if you want to see the messages that people sent to you, just go to www.youtube.com/messages.

You have to take note, however, that if a particular YouTube channel is not connected to Google+, it will not be able to receive messages. The Send Message button will not appear on that channel.

13 Step 11: Choose the Right Camera

Every single one of us knows that creating videos means that you will need a camera since this is what you will be using for shooting the videos.

However, quality is of utmost importance when it comes to filming. People do not like videos with low quality-regardless of how great the content of the video is. Therefore, it is important to use the right camera. If you want to provide your viewers videos with the best quality, then avoid using low-quality cameras. Since most high-end cameras are quite expensive, it is better to look for a good camera that you can afford. You do not necessarily need the ones used by professionals yet-you can start with using digital SLRs. But if you want to use the high-end ones and you have the option to do so, then why not?

14 Step 12: Get the Right Equipment

While it is true that your camera can do practically everything (record the video as well as the audio, automatically set the focus, brightness, etc.), you will also need some other equipment that will help you record videos with better quality. The equipment that you need include a tripod with a pan head which will hold your camera while filming the videos, a light source which will help enhance the quality of your video and a microphone or an audio recorder which will help the camera capture the sounds better.

You will also need extra batteries, most especially if you are going to shoot outside; lens cleaning kit, to get rid of atmospheric pollutants that may affect the clarity of the video; and many more.

15 Step 13: Come Up With Ideas

Even a one-minute video can take a lot of time to produce because the person behind that video does a lot of things prior to the actual filming. They have to start from coming up with ideas as to what video they are going to make.

With millions of videos uploaded on YouTube, it is impossible to come up with a video that haven't been done yet. Some of the most common types of videos that can be found on YouTube are video blogs (or "vlogs"), pet videos, reviews, comedy videos, and montages of video clips, photos and audio. However, that does not mean that the video you are going to produce can no longer be unique, which is why you have to think of creative ideas that will make your video "yours".

16 Step 14: Record Your Video

When recording your video, make sure that you are doing the right thing. Here are some tips that you can take into consideration when filming:

- Do not use digital zoom because the camera uses the highest optical zoom available and then crops the image to a smaller portion of the scene. Therefore, the camcorder is redrawing pixels.
- Make sure that the subject of your videos (i.e. yourself) is properly exposed. You may opt to set the exposure manually, most especially if the subject is backlight.
- Never, ever pan too fast or too slow. If you pan the video too quickly, the details will not be seen. On the other hand, if you pan it too slowly, the video will appear boring.
- Keep your camera steady. Nobody wants to watch a shaky video (unless there is an earthquake in the scene). Therefore, it is important to keep your camera steady to avoid shaking. The most common option that you have is to use a tripod. However, if you do not have a tripod, you can just place your camera on a steady surface like a table.
- Use an external microphone, if you have one. If the sound quality of your video is poor, the overall quality of your video will also be poor. Therefore, it is important to record the sound in excellent quality as well, and an external microphone will most likely help you achieve the desired

audio quality.

17 Step 15: Learn How to Edit Your Video

You can't just take a video and then upload it on your channel without even polishing it. Therefore, aside from knowing how you film your videos, you must also learn how to edit them, which isn't actually that hard. As long as you know how to cut clips, then you already know how to edit videos. Just make sure to cut your raw videos properly-picking the best parts only-and then arrange them all together in the right manner.

Also, keep in mind that while editing software may matter, it does not necessarily mean that your output depends solely on what editor you use. In fact, you don't even have to purchase expensive editing programs. You can just make use of the free software available on the Internet. It's not the matter of what editor you use, it's the matter of how you use it.

18 Step 16: Choose the Right Codec

After editing your video, you now have to consider the video codec (the devices that encode the video when saving and decode when playing it). The quality of your output sometimes depends on which video codec you select. Also, YouTube does not cater to every single codec out there, so you have to be wary in choosing one.

Here are the four video codecs that you can choose from:

- Audio Visual Interleave (AVI), which has some variations, but one of the best AVI video format for Web is the Cinepak Codec by Radius.
- Window Media Video (WMV), which provides clean video at data rates above 340 kbps.
- Motion Picture Experts Group (MPEG/MPG), which also has some variations of this format, but the best one for YouTube is the MPEG4, or the .mp4.
- Apple QuickTime Movie (MOV), which offers clean video at data rates of at least 300 kbps.

19 Step 17: Upload Your Video

After all the things that you have done-from recording the video to editing it-it is safe to say that you can now upload it on YouTube and share it with the rest of the world.

Uploading a video on YouTube is so easy. All you have to do is to click the Upload button at the top of the YouTube page. Afterwards, you can choose the privacy settings of your video prior to uploading it. Select the video that you want to upload and while it is uploading, you can edit the information, such as the title of the video, the description, the tags, the categories, and others. Click Publish to finish uploading the video (if it is a public video), or Done (if it is a private video). YouTube also lets you upload videos using your mobile phones.

20 Step 18: Add Tags on Your Videos

As mentioned in the previous chapter, one of the information that you have to put on your video is the tags, which will help people find it. When the people search for particular keywords related to your tags, your video will appear in their search results.

You must put all relevant and necessary tags on your videos to make them appear in the search results. For instance, if your video is a parody of a particular movie, then you can put tags like the title of the movie itself, the characters of that movie, the actors, and any other things related to that movie. You can even tag "movie", "parody", and the likes. Some people also add popular tags on their videos-regardless whether these tags have something to do with the videos or not-so that these would appear on people's search results.

21 Step 19: Choose the Right Categories for Your Videos

Another thing that you need to put on your video is the category. Just like adding tags on your videos, categorizing your videos is one way of getting them noticed. For example, if your video is a comedy, you can put it in the Comedy categories so that when other people are looking for funny videos to keep them entertained, all they have to do is to browse through the Comedy categories, and then they will be directed to your video.

Moreover, if people see your videos in particular categories frequently, chances are they might even check your channel to see if you still have more videos that they can watch. If they find your videos interesting, they might even subscribe to your channel. Therefore, if you want people to see your videos, you should not forget adding categories to them.

22 Step 20: Write a Good Description for Your Video.

Description is an important part of your video since it basically tells people what your video is all about. This is where you can tell people what to expect from the video. It is a way of telling them that your video is interesting, which is why they have to watch it. While the title for your video can convince them to click on it, your description must be able to convince them to watch it.

Moreover, the description is also one way of making your videos rank better on YouTube, most especially if you put words in there that most people search for. For instance, if you talked about a famous personality on your video and that person's name is in the description, your video will most likely be included in the search results when people search for videos about that person.

23 Step 21: Ask People to Subscribe on Your Channel and Leave Comments

Another factor that will affect the ranking of your videos on YouTube is the channel authority, which can be established with views as well as engagement of your viewers. If your channel is authoritative, you will most likely appear on the top results.

You can establish your authority through the number of subscribers that your channel has, as well as the comments that people leave on your videos. The more subscribers you have, the more your channel will be deemed authoritative since it shows that people like your channel. Moreover, if your videos have many comments, it shows that people liked your videos, or at least watched them until the end. Therefore, it is important to convince your viewers to subscribe on your channel and leave comments on your videos. Comments also let you get feedback from your viewers and let you know whether they liked your videos or not.

24 Step 22: Promote Your YouTube Videos

Promoting your videos is one way of getting noticed on YouTube. You can connect your YouTube channel with your other social media accounts, such as Twitter and Facebook. Once these accounts are already linked, your YouTube updates will automatically be posted on your other social media accounts, and this means that more people will be able to see it. If these people have YouTube accounts, this means that you just earned yourself more subscribers.

You can also ask some of your friends to share your video in their social media accounts. With that, you will be able to reach a much wider range of viewers. If these people really liked your video, then it is most likely that they will also share that to their own set of friends, and then these friends will share your video to their friends. You get the idea.

25 Step 23: Use YouTube for Profit by Being a YouTube Partner

The most common option that people resort to if they want to earn profit through YouTube is joining the YouTube Partner program, in which people are offered the chance to monetize their videos.

Becoming a YouTube partner will not cost you anything. You just have to sign up for the program. Once you are already a partner, Google looks for advertisers that match your videos, decides which advertisements will appear on your videos, monitors all the views or the traffic as well as the ad responses (like when people click on the ad).

Of course, your videos must be eligible for them to be approved for monetization. We will discuss in the next chapter what you should NOT include on your videos. To learn more about YouTube's Partner Program and how you can be a part of it, you can go to www.youtube.com/yt/creators/creator-benefits.html

26 Step 24: Earn Money by Promote Things on Your YouTube Videos

Unless you were born yesterday, you might be aware already that some bloggers make money just by, you know, blogging. Some companies or businesses hire these bloggers to blog about their products in exchange for a payment.

Essentially, creating videos on YouTube is just like creating a blog, but in video form (which is why they are called "vlogs"). You create your own content. You have the control as to what your videos will be all about.

If you want to earn money out of creating YouTube videos, one thing you can do aside from being a YouTube partner is promote through your videos. You can create videos for a particular business or company that will promote their products and services. You can upload these videos on your YouTube channel and in turn get paid.

27 Step 25: Comply With the Rules and Play It Safe

Your videos will not be considered eligible if you use contents that you didn't create yourself or at least didn't get the permission of the creator to use it. If you used other people's contents for your video, you must be able to present written permission for the audio, the visuals, and other contents that are just not yours.

YouTube is very strict when it comes to this matter, which means that you have to be careful when using elements in your video that are not yours. Some examples of videos that are not eligible include those that contain a song purchased for personal use and did not get commercial license, or singing words of a copyrighted song and there is a copyrighted audio in the background.

28 Step 26: Avoid Copyright Infringement

Copyright is very important for the whole YouTube community. Basically, copyright refers to the ownership of a work that a person created by him or herself. The said owner has all the rights to use that work in particular ways that he or she wants to. Of course, when you put all your efforts to a particular work, you don't want other people to just steal it from you, do you? It does not mean that you are being selfish; it just means that you deserve the credits for your hard work.

Once YouTube finds out that you use a copyrighted content on your video without getting the permission of the person who owns the copyright of that content, the upload of your video may not push through. If you repeatedly commit copyright infringement, your YouTube account will be permanently terminated. You can learn about copyright on YouTube by visiting www.youtube.com/yt/copyright.

29 Step 27: Be Wary of Your Identity on YouTube

YouTube-just like any other websites on the Internet-is a public space. If your account is public, anyone on the Internet can see what you put there. Therefore, you must be wary of what you upload on YouTube. Always make sure that you do not reveal too much in your videos as well as in your channel. You must also be cautious when it comes to sharing some confidential information, such as your full name as well as your location or address. You should also think twice before you give your email address. You may want to create an email address solely for your YouTube account where people can send you messages, most especially if these messages are business-related. You can also just suggest that they send you private message through YouTube.

30 Step 28: Get Inspiration From Successful YouTubers

Many professional authors out there say that reading is important if you want to be good in writing. You should expose yourself to what is out there to get an idea as to what you should do.

This very same principle also applies to YouTube. If you want to get an idea as to what you should do, you have to expose yourself to what is out there. Watch videos that uploaded by successful and professional YouTubers. Get an idea as to what they do in their videos, as well as what their techniques are. Getting inspiration from other YouTubers may give you an idea as to how you can be successful as well. And hey, it doesn't hurt if you will watch other people's videos. In fact, it can also be entertaining since these people are usually those who produce the best videos on YouTube. Who knows, maybe next time you are already one of them!

31 Step 29: Consider People's Feedback

You are just casually browsing through the comments on one of your videos until you read a comment that says something like "your video wasn't shot very well" or "what a waste of time." While this can be hurtful, consider this comment as constructive, which will help you improve your future videos.

Since you are just new, you can't expect yourself to have the best YouTube video ever. In fact, it is most likely that your video isn't that great as compared to others'. If some people leave comments on your video saying that it is not that good, consider those comments as feedback that will help you improve in the future. For instance, if one person says that the background music that you used is too loud, take note of that feedback to make sure that the background music on your next video will no longer be just as loud. Consider people's feedback, even though they are negative because it will most likely help improve your work.

32 Step 30: Expand Your Knowledge About YouTube

It is also important to expand your knowledge about YouTube. It's not enough that you only know how to upload a video and leave a comment on someone else's video. There are still a lot of things out there that you should familiarize yourself with. You can let's say start with understanding YouTube's policies. Read books about YouTube (good thing you have this book!). Browse the internet and read articles. Look for tips on how you can be a successful YouTuber. Browse YouTube. Know what some features are for.

If you don't know something, just look around the Internet and you will most likely find the answers that you are looking for. You can also join forums and discussions together with other YouTubers so that you can learn more about how everything works. You can also go to YouTube Help Center where you can find practically everything that you need to know about YouTube.

33 Step 31: Have Fun With What You Are Doing

You might have already encountered this saying before "Choose a job you love, and you will never have to work a day in your life."

I know we will all agree with this: there is nothing better than having fun with what you are doing. Just because creating videos for YouTube requires a lot of effort and hard work, it does not mean that you should already sacrifice having fun while doing it. Don't take everything way too seriously up to the point when you are no longer having fun. Most people setup a YouTube channel primarily because they just want to have fun doing it (earning money is just a bonus). If you are having fun with running your YouTube channel, you will not get tired of creating videos and sharing them to other people all over the world.

34 Closing Thoughts

I hope you enjoyed the read and found what you were looking for. If so, I'd like to ask you for a favor: Please, take a moment to **review my book on Amazon!** Thanks.

Thank you for getting "31 Steps to a Better YouTube Channel" and I wish you all the best with your YouTube Channel. May you get hundreds of thousands of subscribers!

If you would like to get updates about special offers and new books from me or see my other books, please visit my author profile at our publisher:

publishedok.com/pv

Philip vang

Author

35 Preview of "31 Steps to Minimalism"

Preview chapter of "31 Steps to Minimalism: The Joy of Less and Reclaiming Your Life to Be Easy and De-Cluttered. Go Back to a Simple Life, Full of Fun and De-Stressed":

A creative mind is one of the requirements to a minimalist mind set. Creativity is also involved in the process of learning your new skills - living a minimalist life.

Most consumers make the mistake of paying for goods and services at an unnecessarily premium amount just to save effort and time. For instance, they will stop at their favorite fast food establishments to pick-up dinner after a long day's work. If you are going to compute for the money you are going to save - you will realize you have a lot. You pay too much on food and at the same time, you are consuming unhealthy food which leads to different illnesses and diseases.

You become a minimalist by devoting time to learn how to prepare your own food. Simply watch online videos or television shows, or read cook books. You can improve your cooking skills if you will devote at least five to 10 minutes to read and learn a new dish. As a result, you unleash your creativity by enhancing your cooking skills and eating healthier dishes because you carefully plan your meals. Plus, you get to save on time otherwise spent to get to a fast food restaurant. ...

Preview of the Table of Contents of "31 Steps to Minimalism":

- Understand the Real Meaning of Minimalist Life
- Know the Four Basic Concepts of Minimalism
- Shift Your Mind Set
- You Possess the Things You Need
- Stop Buying Unnecessary Items
- Be Happy in Doing and Not Owning
- Learn When You Have Enough
- Keep Positive Surroundings
- Avoid Advertisements
- Spend Time for Vacation
- Start Building a Happy Home

To check out the rest of 31 Steps to Minimalism: The Joy of Less and Reclaiming Your Life to Be Easy and De-Cluttered. Go Back to a Simple Life, Full of Fun and De-Stressed" please go to the following link:

bit.ly/31minimal

36 Preview of "31 Steps to Become a Vegan"

Preview chapter of "31 Steps to Become a Vegan: It Is Not Just About the Food. You Want to Be Healthy, Fit and Change Your Diet. Here Is How You Do It.":

A great way to start off your vegan plan of action is to ease into it. This will make the choice much easier, if the adjustment is made not abruptly, but gradually. The transition of your body will also be easy. Any sudden, drastic change in your diet will affect your body tremendously, especially changes in being an omnivore to becoming a full-pledged vegan.

One thing to remember is to listen to what your body is telling you and avoid forcing yourself to change everything completely without proper guidance and information. You may start by removing cheese, then eggs, then milk and dairy products, then meat. It is also advisable to remove one type of animal from your diet at a time. One can also start with being vegetarian, then removing eggs and dairy eventually. The most important thing is to go at your own pace. You may also begin with one thing that you consume the most, and then start substituting with the vegan version.

For instance, if you drink milk every day, you may begin substituting it with almond milk. One great way of doing it is taking into account all the junk food in your home, such as anything with refined flour, sugar and processed food. One may target one type of junk food and start with a healthier vegan option. If you have potato chips and cheese dip, why not have some nacho cheese and salsa. If you like candy, why not eat apples and bananas?

It takes months, even years to build a habit, so a gradual approach is always the better choice. Going cold turkey is like setting yourself up for failure.

Preview of the Table of Contents of "31 Steps to Become a Vegan":

- Research and Plan Your Vegan Journey
- Start It Right
- Know What Vegans Eat
- Eating and Cooking Vegan Good
- Living Vegan
- Sustaining the Vegan Lifestyle

To check out the rest of 31 Steps to Become a Vegan: It Is Not Just About the Food. You Want to Be Healthy, Fit and Change Your Diet. Here Is How You Do It." please go to the following link:

bit.ly/31vegan

37 Preview of "31 Steps to Start a Business"

PHILIP VANG

Preview chapter of "31 Steps to Start a Business: From Finding Your Passion to Going Out There to Do It, This Ultimate Guide Will Help You Figure Out the Steps to Build Your Own Business and Future. Start Working for Yourself!":

In managing a business, there lies a huge difference between "you have to" and "you want to". The first one dictates that you are obliged to accomplish something even if you see no reason of doing it. You are forced to complete a task that in return, produces poor outcomes. Mediocre outputs may mean downfall to the business since the customers always want the best products and services.

In order to generate better results, doing what you want helps you achieve this goal. Recognizing your passions can definitely help you attain success in your endeavor. Additionally, identifying the purpose of your business can aid you in continuing what you have established. Reminding of yourself why you started in the first place may inspire you to carry on with your venture. In the long run, you will realize that managing a business is easier when you are motivated.

Preview of the Table of Contents of "31 Steps to Start a Business":

- Evaluating Yourself
- Identifying Your Passion
- Establishing Your Goal
- Devising Your Business Plan
- Choosing Your Business Structure
- Recognizing Your Target Market
- Calculating the Costs
- Fixing Your Budget
- Gathering Your Resources
- Obtaining a Place of Work

To check out the rest of 31 Steps to Start a Business: From Finding Your Passion to Going Out There to Do It, This Ultimate Guide Will Help You Figure Out the Steps to Build Your Own Business and Future. Start Working for Yourself!" please go to the following link:

bit.ly/31business

13750646R00047

Printed in Poland
by Amazon Fulfillment
Poland Sp. z o.o., Wrocław